Little Science

Match Mom and Cub

By Amanda Gebhardt

2 Match this cub and its mom.

This cub has four legs.

4 It has a long tail, too.

This cub has fur. It is small.

6 It will grow. Its mom will be big.

This mom is big. But her
tail is short.

 This mom has a long tail. Is this its mom? How can you tell?

Oh! This is its mom.
Its mom has no spots.

This cub has lots of spots.

Mom and cub are the
same in other ways.

Look and see what is the same.

Mom and cub like
when they play!

Word List

science words

cub	Mom
fur	same
grow	spots
mom	tail

sight words

a	her	short
are	How	small
be	no	the
four	of	what
fur	other	

Vowel Teams

/ā/ai, ay, ey	/ē/ee	/ō/oh, ow	/o͞o/oo, ou	/o͝o/oo
play	see	grow	too	Look
tail		Oh	you	
they				
ways				

Try It!

Look at pictures of baby animals and their mom or dad. Tell how they are the same. Tell how they are different.

94 Words

Match this cub and its mom.

This cub has four legs.

It has a long tail, too.

This cub has fur. It is small.

It will grow. Its mom will be big.

This mom is big. But her tail is short.

This mom has a long tail. Is this its mom? How can you tell?

Oh! This is its mom. Its mom has no spots.

This cub has lots of spots.

Mom and cub are the same in other ways.

Look and see what is the same.

Mom and cub like when they play!

CHERRY BLOSSOM PRESS

Published in the United States of America by Cherry Lake Publishing Group
Ann Arbor, Michigan
www.cherrylakepublishing.com

Photo Credits: © Volodymyr Burdiak/Shutterstock, cover, title page; © iva/Shutterstock, 2; © iva/Shutterstock, 3; © Chris Desborough/Shutterstock, 4; © Geoffrey Kuchera/Shutterstock, 5; © James Roy/Shutterstock, 6; © Giedriius/Shutterstock, 7; © Debbie Steinhausser/Shutterstock, 8; © Evelyn D. Harrison/Shutterstock, 9; © outdoorsman/Shutterstock, 10; © Danita Delimont/Shutterstock, 11; © Danita Delimont/Shutterstock, 12; © Chris Desborough/Shutterstock, 13; © Eric Isselee/Shutterstock, back cover

Cherry Blossom Press is an imprint of Cherry Lake Publishing Group.

Library of Congress Cataloging-in-Publication Data

Names: Gebhardt, Amanda, author.
Title: Match mom and cub / written by Amanda Gebhardt.
Description: Ann Arbor, Michigan : Cherry Blossom Press, [2024] | Series:
   Little science stories | Audience: Grades K-1 | Summary: "Explore how
   animals and their offspring are the same and different in this decodable
   science book for beginning readers. A combination of domain-specific
   sight words and sequenced phonics skills builds confidence in content
   area reading. Bold, colorful photographs align directly with the text to
   help readers strengthen comprehension"— Provided by publisher.
Identifiers: LCCN 2023035049 | ISBN 9781668937655 (paperback) | ISBN
   9781668940037 (ebook) | ISBN 9781668941386 (pdf)
Subjects: LCSH: Animals—Infancy—Juvenile literature. | Parental behavior
   in animals—Juvenile literature.
Classification: LCC QL763 .G43 2024 | DDC 591.3/92—dc23/eng/20230905
LC record available at https://lccn.loc.gov/2023035049

Printed in the United States of America

Amanda Gebhardt is a curriculum writer and editor and a life-long learner. She lives in Ann Arbor, Michigan, with her husband, two kids, and one playful pup named Cookie.